FRENCH
VEGETARIAN
COOKING

IN A NUTSHELL

FRENCH VEGETARIAN COOKING

A STEP-BY-STEP GUIDE

MARIE-PIERRE MOINE

ELEMENT

SHAFTESBURY, DORSET • BOSTON, MASSACHUSETTS • MELBOURNE, VICTORIA

© Element Books Limited 1999

First published in
Great Britain in 1999 by
ELEMENT BOOKS LIMITED
Shaftesbury, Dorset SP7 8BP

Published in the USA in 1999 by
ELEMENT BOOKS INC
160 North Washington Street, Boston
MA 02114

Published in Australia in 1999 by
ELEMENT BOOKS LIMITED
and distributed by Penguin Australia Ltd
487 Maroondah Highway, Ringwood,
Victoria 3134

NOTE FROM THE PUBLISHER
Unless specified otherwise
All recipes serve four
All eggs are medium
All herbs are fresh
All spoon measurements are level
Tablespoon = 15ml spoon
Teaspoon = 5ml spoon
Both metric and Imperial
measurements have been given. To
ensure success, when making a recipe,
follow one set of measurements only;
do not mix them.

Designed and created with Element Books
by The Bridgewater Book Company Ltd.

ELEMENT BOOKS LIMITED
Managing Editor Miranda Spicer
Senior Commissioning Editor Caro Ness
Editor Finny Fox-Davies
Group Production Director Clare Armstrong
Production Controller Claire Legg

THE BRIDGEWATER BOOK
COMPANY
Art Director Terry Jeavons
Design and page layout by Axis Design
Editor Jo Wells
Project Editor Caroline Earle
Photography David Jordan
Home Economy Judy Williams
Picture Research Caroline Thomas

Printed and bound in Portugal
by Printer Portuguesa.

British Library Cataloguing in Publication
data available

ISBN 1 86204 382 5

*The publishers wish to thank the following for
the use of pictures:*
Tony Stone Images pp.6, 9.

Contents

Traditional French cooking

AS MANY DESPAIRING *vegetarian tourists in France will be only too quick to point out, France is not a country that is readily associated with vegetarian cooking. Look at the menus of all those nice little restaurants and you won't see much in the way of vegetarian dishes. Unless you are very lucky, you will have to make do with yet another* omelette *or* salade de tomates.

However, local markets in towns and villages throughout the country abound with stalls heaped with bright, tempting vegetables and fruit, fresh nuts, gleaming olives and tiny dried beans. So, to enjoy French vegetarian cooking, you have to cook for yourself or eat in private homes with French families who are not trying to impress customers with elaborate meat or fish

BELOW *Vegetarian food features in French family cooking.*

TRADITIONAL FRENCH COOKING

component of country meals and have remained a favourite for supper. Salads are eaten on a daily basis, as starters or to cleanse the palate after a main course. Vegetables are prepared carefully and given pride of place, frequently as a separate course. They are presented attractively and often finished with fresh herbs. New-season produce is eagerly awaited and discussed; people go out of their way to buy early asparagus, baby artichokes or the first strawberries of the year, and are happy to pay extra for them.

ABOVE *A hearty vegetable soup can make a main course.*

dishes. Traditional, French everyday home cooking makes full use of the vegetables and fruit that look so stunning in markets everywhere. The tradition of carefully cooking vegetables and pulses goes back a long way, to the days when meat and poultry were kept for high days and holidays and were not part of the average everyday diet.

USING VEGETABLES
Vegetables do have an important part to play in the typical French menu. Soups were the main

ABOVE *A salad makes a light and appetizing start to a meal.*

Nutrition and choosing vegetables

A HEALTHY VEGETARIAN DIET *that supplies the body's nutritional needs is composed of a mixture of carbohydrates, protein, vitamins, minerals and fat in the right amounts and combinations.*

To obtain all of the essential nutrients, fresh vegetables and fruit should be supplemented with grains, pulses, dairy products, nuts and seeds. Try to combine cheese dishes with a salad, and/or lightly steamed or boiled vegetables. Refined foods that are high in saturated fat, additives, excessive salt and sugar should be avoided. If using any additional fat, stick to the traditional fat of the Mediterranean, olive oil, preferably extra virgin and cold pressed for maximum nutrients, and use it in very small amounts.

ABOVE **A cheese omelette with salad makes a balanced meal.**

LEFT **Extra virgin olive oil is the healthiest fat to use**

BE CHOOSY

When it comes to selecting vegetables for a diet that will be enjoyable as well as healthy, the secret is to behave like the French when visiting food markets, supermarkets or greengrocers and to be very

choosy. Seek fresh-looking vegetables: green vegetables should be green, never brown or yellowing; tomatoes should be a rich red colour, not pale orange-pink; and the skin of onions and garlic should not look like old papyrus. For both health and taste reasons, buy organic produce whenever you can. At present, the range available is often limited, but the more demand there is, the more attractive the choice, availability and prices are likely to become.

ABOVE *Feel produce before you buy it to test for ripeness.*

Another tip to learn from the French, which may not make you very popular but is worth putting into practice, is to feel vegetables to check that they are firm and have a bit of bounce, rather than being rock solid or soft and flabby.

With a few exceptions, such as avocados and bananas which go on ripening at room temperature and so can be bought unripe, buy little and often so that produce is eaten at its freshest. In this way you will be able to get the best from your food not just in terms of taste, but in essential vitamins and nutrients.

Herbs and spices

FRENCH COOKING RELIES *a great deal on herbs to complement or bring out the flavours of the ingredients. Spices are used less frequently, but to great effect.*

HERBS

The three most popular herbs in French cooking are parsley, thyme and bay leaves, often combined as the basis of a bouquet garni. Thyme and bay leaves are sturdy herbs and are excellent dried; rosemary, marjoram and oregano dry

PARSLEY

well, but parsley loses flavour in the drying process and is best fresh or frozen. The best way to have a ready supply of parsley is to grow it in a

THYME

sheltered spot in a garden or in a pot on the window sill, but if this is not possible, then buy it fresh from a supermarket or greengrocer.

BAY LEAVES

1 Snip the amount of leaves that are needed for the dish being prepared; use the stalks to flavour soups and casseroles.

2 Surplus parsley can be snipped finely and put in a small bag in the freezer.

3 Shake out a little frozen snipped parsley when required – contact with warm or room temperature food will thaw it very quickly.

4 Chives, basil, tarragon and coriander can be used in the same way. Delicate chervil is best used fresh.

RIGHT **Whole roasted garlic adds an irresistible fragrance to any dish.**

SPICES

Spices such as cumin, cinnamon, nutmeg, paprika and precious saffron are used discreetly in French cooking. Buy in small amounts, store in a cool, dark, dry place and use within 6 months.

GARLIC

Don't keep garlic for too long and discard any cloves that are soft or start sprouting green shoots. Take great care not to let garlic burn; it will taste very acrid and spoil the dish.

GARLIC CLOVES

Preparation and cooking techniques

THE TRADITIONAL *French kitchen is 'low tech', retaining simple and sensible basic cooking techniques that achieve wonderful results.*

RINSING

Exceptions to the rinsing rule are raspberries and similar berries, which should just be checked for foreign bodies, and mushrooms which are best wiped with damp kitchen paper.

1 Rinse all fruit and vegetables thoroughly unless they are to be boiled, poached or steamed. Drain well and dry with a tea towel or kitchen paper.

BLANCHING

This quick and useful process involves plunging ingredients into boiling water for about 1–3 minutes to soften them and prepare them for further cooking, then cooling quickly.

1 To peel tomatoes, make a cross in the rounded ends and plunge into boiling water for about 1 minute. To peel a peach, slit the skin at the rounded end and plunge into boiling water for 2–4 minutes, depending on ripeness.

SAUTÉEING

This favourite cooking method is done in a frying pan or a slightly deeper sauté pan.

1 Rub the pan with oil, then put on a medium to high heat and melt a little butter in it. Add the main ingredients.

2 Classically, the pan is tossed and shaken to keep the food moving, but in French homes the food is usually fried and stirred occasionally.

3 To make a little sauce, remove the cooked ingredients and keep them warm. Pour a little water, wine or fruit juice into the pan and leave to bubble for 1 minute. For a glossy sauce, whisk in a knob of butter or two teaspoons of cream.

STEAMING

When steaming, make sure that the steamer or colander is not in contact with the water, and check from time to time that the water hasn't boiled away.

1 Place the food in the top of the steamer and cover it tightly so that no steam escapes. A layer of foil will help if the lid does not fit well.

2 Two layers of foil tightly enclosing the steamer can be used to replace a lid.

BLANCHED AND PEELED GARLIC

This makes garlic easier on the palate and minimizes its occasional side effects.

1 Bring unpeeled garlic cloves to the boil in a saucepan of cold water, then simmer for about 5–8 minutes, depending on the size of the cloves.

2 Drain and refresh under cold water. When cool enough to handle, squeeze the cloves gently between the thumb and index finger and the garlic flesh will come out easily. Use as required.

CHARRED AND PEELED PEPPERS

1 Cook peppers halved lengthways, cut side down, under a preheated hot grill until the skin is charred and blistered.

2 Leave until cool enough to handle, then peel away the skins using a sharp knife.

CROÛTONS

1 To make large, oven-dried croûtons to serve with soups and stews, rub the cut sides of a halved garlic clove over thin slices of left-over baguette-style bread and brush them lightly with olive oil.

2 Bake for 5–8 minutes at 190°C/375°F/gas mark 5 on the coolest shelf of the oven, or until golden and crisp.

3 To make bite-size crunchy croûtons to add to salads, rub a frying pan with the cut side of a garlic clove and place over a medium heat.

4 Add 1 tablespoon olive oil or 2 teaspoons oil and a small knob of butter. When hot, add cubes of day-old bread and cook, stirring frequently, for about 2–3 minutes, or until golden. Drain on kitchen paper and cool. Keep in an airtight container for 3–4 days.

The Storecupboard

IN ADDITION TO FRESH VEGETABLES, *fruit and bread, to cook in the French style keep your kitchen stocked with a range of good quality oils, vinegars and preserved and canned goods.*

ITEMS TO HAVE IN STOCK

Rice

Pasta

Bulgar wheat, couscous or semolina

Small green Le Puy lentils

Flour

Tabasco

Canned tomatoes

Honey

Canned flageolet or cannellini beans

Vegetable stock cubes or bouillon cubes

Dijon mustard

Wholegrain mustard

Groundnut or sunflower oil

Olive oil (preferably extra virgin)

Walnut oil

Red and white wine vinegar

Sherry vinegar

Sea salt and coarse sea salt

Black pepper for grinding freshly as needed

Redcurrant preserve

Walnuts and almonds

PASTA

DIJON MUSTARD

LE PUY LENTILS

SEA SALT

STOCK CUBES

WALNUTS

Hazelnuts
and pine
nuts

Lemons

Oranges

Black olives
in brine

Spanish
onions

Shallots

Garlic

LEMONS

CAPERS

Capers

Butter (unsalted
or lightly salted)

Cream or fromage frais

Parmesan cheese

Red and white wine

WHITE WINE

BELOW **A selection of ingredients from
the French storecupboard. It is always
worth buying the best quality you can
afford and checking the 'use-by' dates on
a regular basis to ensure freshness.**

OLIVE OIL

SHERRY VINEGAR

WALNUT OIL

CREAM   BUTTER

COUSCOUS

AUBERGINE

GARLIC

TOMATO

LE PUY LENTILS   HARD CHEESE   GOATS' CHEESE   MIXED FRESH HERBS

RED PEPPER

COURGETTES

17

Crudités with Two Sauces

THIS IS AN EASY STARTER *or snack to prepare. The herb sauce and mayonnaise can be made and chilled in advance and the prepared vegetables kept covered in a cool place for 1 hour.*

INGREDIENTS

FOR THE CRUDITÉS

Selection of raw vegetables: carrots, red, yellow and green peppers, cucumber and celery, cut into fine strips; cauliflower and broccoli, divided into florets; cherry tomatoes, radishes and small button mushrooms, left whole

FOR THE GARLIC MAYONNAISE

2 egg yolks
1 tsp red or white wine vinegar
½ tsp hot mustard
2 garlic cloves, crushed
175ml (6fl oz) groundnut oil
120ml (4fl oz) olive oil
salt and freshly ground black pepper
few drops of lemon juice

FOR THE HERB SAUCE

115g (4oz) fromage frais
1 garlic clove, crushed
*2 spring onions,
white parts only, chopped*
1 shallot, finely chopped
small bunch of chives
few sprigs of flat leaf parsley

1 To make the garlic mayonnaise, put the egg yolks, vinegar, mustard and garlic in a covered bowl and set aside for 5–10 minutes.

2 Place the bowl on damp kitchen paper so it doesn't slip. Using an electric whisk, mix the ingredients well. Whisking constantly, add the oils, a drop at a time at first, then a few drops at a time.

5 Arrange the vegetables around the bowls of mayonnaise and herb sauce.

3 As soon as the mixture begins to thicken, dribble in the oil a little faster, still whisking constantly. Season with pepper and lemon juice. Cover and chill.

4 To make the green herb sauce, mash the fromage frais with a fork. Mix in the garlic, spring onions and shallot. Snip in the chives and parsley. Stir together, then season. Refrigerate for at least 30 minutes before serving, but eat the same day.

COOK'S TIP

To help prevent the mayonnaise from separating during storage, beat 1 tablespoon boiling water into the sauce.

Grated Carrot Salad with Hazelnuts

THIS COLOURFUL SALAD *is a perfect starter for a winter meal, and a great way to make carrots appealing to young children.*

INGREDIENTS

400g (14oz) mature carrots, grated

2 tbsp olive oil

2 tbsp mayonnaise

1 tbsp lemon juice

1 tbsp orange juice

handful of hazelnuts

a few chives or flat leaf parsley leaves

salt and freshly ground black pepper

CHIVES

VARIATIONS

- For a main course salad, add wedges of hard-boiled egg.

- Add a few black olives, pitted and coarsely chopped, raisins or chopped cheese.

- For extra crunch, add some shredded white cabbage.

1 Put the carrots in a large bowl. Combine the oil, mayonnaise and lemon and orange juices. Season to taste with salt and pepper.

2 Pour over the carrots and toss until well coated. Leave at room temperature for at least 10 minutes, or chill the mixture for several hours in the refrigerator.

3 If time allows, dry-fry the hazelnuts in a non-stick frying pan over a medium heat for 2–3 minutes, or until lightly browned. If not, use the nuts as they are.

4 Just before serving, toss the hazelnuts into the salad and snip in the herbs.

CARROTS

Cucumber Salad

SALTING CUCUMBERS DRAWS *out the juices, a process known as* dégorging, *making them tender in texture and easier to digest.*

INGREDIENTS

1 large cucumber
4½ tsp coarse sea salt
several sprigs of tarragon
1 tbsp lemon juice
2–3 tbsp crème fraîche
freshly ground black pepper
snipped tarragon, to garnish

1 Pare off strips of skin lengthways at intervals around the cucumber and thinly slice. Layer with salt in a colander. Cover with a weighted plate. Leave for 30 minutes.

2 Rinse well in cold water, drain and squeeze dry. Finish drying with kitchen paper.

3 Place in a bowl. Snip over the tarragon and sprinkle with lemon juice. Mix well.

4 Add the crème fraîche; toss well. Season with pepper. Chill for at least 10 minutes.

Green Salad with Walnuts

FOR MOST FRENCH PEOPLE, *no meal is complete without a lightly dressed green salad to cleanse the palate after the main course.*

INGREDIENTS

200g (7oz) Cos or lamb's lettuce
½ garlic clove
6–8 walnuts, shelled
salt and freshly ground black pepper
2 tsp red wine vinegar
3 tbsp walnut oil
1 tbsp groundnut oil

3 Place the prepared salad leaves on top of the dressing but do not toss. Just before serving, toss lightly to coat the leaves in the dressing. Stir in the remaining walnuts.

1 Separate the salad leaves and cut in half if large. Rinse, drain and dry well.

2 Rub a bowl with the cut side of the garlic. Add half the walnuts and the vinegar, season and stir. Beat in the oils.

Potato and Watercress Soup

THE POTATO MAKES *this hearty soup surprisingly creamy. For extra glossy richness, add a knob of butter in step four.*

INGREDIENTS

2 waxy potatoes, each about 175g (6oz), chopped

salt and freshly ground black pepper

2 tsp oil

350g (12oz) trimmed watercress

pinch of freshly grated nutmeg

4½ tsp single cream, yogurt or fromage frais, to serve

VARIATION

Spinach and spring greens are good alternatives to watercress.

WATERCRESS

POTATO AND WATERCRESS SOUP

1 Stir the potatoes in the oil in a heavy saucepan over a medium heat for 1 minute. Add enough boiling water to cover, bring to a simmer and cook for about 10 minutes.

2 Add the watercress, reserving a few sprigs, and the nutmeg. Cook for about 5 minutes, or until the vegetables are tender.

4 Mix a little hot water in the blender or food processor to rinse, pour into the soup and adjust the consistency with more hot water, if necessary.

5 Reheat, then pour into warm soup bowls. Swirl in a little cream, yogurt or fromage frais and garnish with the reserved watercress. Season with extra pepper.

3 Cool slightly, then process in a blender or food processor. Return to the pan.

NUTMEG

Provençale Soup

THIS CHUNKY SOUP *is a meal in itself. The richly flavoured sauce of basil, garlic and egg, known as* pistou, *makes it extra special.*

INGREDIENTS

1 large red onion, chopped

2 garlic cloves, crushed

1 tbsp olive oil

400g (14oz) can chopped tomatoes and their juice

300g (11oz) courgettes, chopped

1 carrot, chopped

3 tbsp fresh or frozen shelled broad beans

100g (3 ½oz) small macaroni

225g (8oz) can haricot beans, drained

50g (2oz) Gruyère or mature Cheddar cheese, grated

salt and freshly ground black pepper

croûtons, to serve (see page 15)

FOR THE SAUCE

1 large egg, boiled for 3½ minutes

1 tsp wine vinegar

150ml (¼ pint) olive oil

3½ tsp single cream

several sprigs of flat leaf parsley

several basil leaves

1 Cook the onion and garlic in the oil in a heavy-based saucepan over a medium heat for 2–3 minutes. Add the tomatoes and their juice, together with the vegetables. Cover with boiling water, stir and bring to the boil.

COOK'S TIP

Any leftover sauce will keep for a couple of days, covered, in the refrigerator. Use as a dressing for crisp lettuce or as a sauce with boiled potatoes.

2 Sprinkle in the pasta and add 500ml (18fl oz) boiling water; the pasta will absorb the water as it cooks. Return to a simmer. Cook for about 10 minutes, or until the pasta is just tender. Add the haricot beans, reduce the heat to very low. Season.

3 Meanwhile, make the sauce. Scoop the egg yolk into a bowl; reserve the white. Beat the yolk with a pinch of salt and the vinegar. Beat in the oil in a thin trickle with an electric whisk. Then beat in the cream to make a thin sauce.

4 Mash the egg white and stir into the sauce. Snip in parsley and basil and add plenty of pepper. Serve the soup with the cheese, croûtons and sauce.

GARLIC

Shallot and Mushroom Soup

SHALLOTS AND MUSHROOMS *simmered with stock and wine make this version of the bistro classic pleasantly light and piquant.*

INGREDIENTS

*5 large spring onions,
white parts only, chopped*

4 shallots, chopped

2 tsp groundnut or sunflower oil

25g (1oz) butter

*150g (5oz) chestnut mushrooms,
thinly sliced*

350ml (12fl oz) vegetable stock

120ml (4fl oz) white wine

6 small slices of baguette

*50g (2oz) Gruyère or Emmental
cheese, grated*

freshly ground black pepper

Serves 2

1 Cook the chopped spring onions and shallots in the oil in a heavy-based saucepan over a medium heat, stirring frequently, for 2–3 minutes, or until lightly coloured. Add the butter and mushrooms, increase the heat slightly and cook for a further 5 minutes.

VARIATION

In Step 4, break an egg into each bowl before adding the broth and cheese croûtons. The eggs will poach under the grill.

CHESTNUT
MUSHROOMS

2 Add the stock and wine and bring to the boil. Reduce the heat, cover and simmer gently for at least 10 minutes (preferably a little longer to allow the flavours to develop fully).

4 Using a slotted spoon, divide the cooked vegetables between 2 heatproof bowls. Pour in the broth and top with the bread, cheese side up. Grill until the cheese bubbles. Serve piping hot.

3 Meanwhile, spread the cheese over the bread, taking it to the edges. Season with pepper.

SHALLOTS

Spinach Soufflé

SOUFFLÉS ARE *at their most enjoyable when the inside is wobbly or even slightly gooey and the outside golden brown and crisp.*

INGREDIENTS

*45g (1½oz) butter, plus extra
for greasing*

25g (1oz) plain flour

200ml (7fl oz) milk

*75g (3oz) Gruyère or mature Cheddar
cheese, grated*

*250g (9oz) small spinach
leaves, shredded*

3 large eggs, separated

a pinch of nutmeg

1 extra large egg white

salt and freshly ground black pepper

**Serves 2 as a main dish,
4 as a starter**

VARIATIONS

● To make individual soufflés, use two 15cm (6in) or four 10cm (4in) soufflé dishes. Reduce the cooking time by 8–12 minutes.

● To make a plain cheese soufflé, omit the spinach and increase the cheese by 25g (1oz). Mashed blue cheese is a delicious alternative to grated Gruyère or Cheddar.

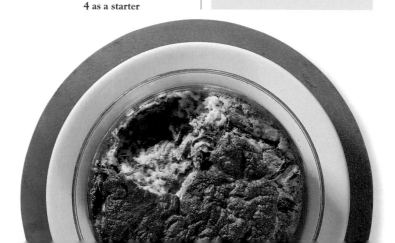

1 Melt 25g (1oz) of the butter in a heavy-based saucepan over a medium heat. Stir in the flour until absorbed. Gradually add the milk, beating well. Beat until bubbling. Reduce the heat and simmer, beating occasionally, for 3–4 minutes. Cool briefly and add the cheese.

2 Wilt the spinach in the remaining butter in a frying pan over a medium heat. Add to the sauce with the egg yolks, nutmeg and seasoning.

3 Whisk the whites to soft peaks. Fold a few spoonfuls into the sauce, using a spatula or large metal spoon. Lightly, but thoroughly, fold the remaining egg whites into the sauce.

4 Pour into a generously buttered 850ml (1½ pint) soufflé dish, about 15cm (6in) diameter. Bake in a preheated oven at 190°C/375°F/gas 5 for 20–25 minutes, or until well risen and browned, but moist inside. Serve immediately.

Tomato Tart

UNLIKE A QUICHE, *this tart contains neither cream nor eggs. It is the savoury equivalent of a classic French fruit tart.*

INGREDIENTS

225g (8oz) shortcrust pastry

900g (2lb) ripe tomatoes, thinly sliced

1 garlic clove, crushed

2 tsp dried thyme

1 tsp dried marjoram or oregano

2 tsp caster sugar

salt and freshly ground black pepper

2 tbsp olive oil

25g (1oz) butter

15g (½oz) freshly grated
Parmesan cheese

basil leaves, to garnish

**Serves 4 as a light lunch
or 6 as a starter**

1 Roll out the pastry on a lightly floured surface and use to line a buttered loose-based 23cm (9in) flan tin. Chill in the refrigerator for 20–30 minutes.

2 Cook the tomatoes sprinkled with the garlic, herbs, sugar and seasoning, in the oil and 20g (¾oz) of the butter in a large frying pan over a medium heat for about 5 minutes, then turn over, reduce the heat a little and cook for another 5–10 minutes.

4 Prick the pastry base with a fork, cover with foil and raw rice or baking beans and bake on a hot baking sheet in a preheated oven at 200°C/ 400°F/gas 6 for 10 minutes. Cool slightly. Remove the foil and rice or beans.

5 Sprinkle the Parmesan over the pastry. Arrange the tomatoes on top in overlapping circles, starting from the outside. Dot with the remaining butter and bake for 15–20 minutes, or until golden and bubbling. Serve warm garnished with basil.

3 Carefully transfer the tomatoes to a colander set over a bowl to drain. Use the juices in a sauce or soup.

COOK'S TIP

If the pastry browns too quickly, cover loosely with crumpled foil.

Asparagus with Lemon Butter

USE THIN GREEN ASPARAGUS, *which is easier to find and prepare and less expensive than French white or purple asparagus.*

INGREDIENTS

450g (1lb) thinnish green asparagus

salt and freshly ground black pepper

50g (2oz) unsalted butter, diced

4½ tsp lemon juice

ASPARAGUS WITH LEMON BUTTER

1 Bring 5cm (2in) salted water to the boil in a large saucepan, add the asparagus and simmer for 4–5 minutes, or until just tender.

2 Lift from the pan with a fish slice or tongs. Drain. Tip the water from the pan. Return the pan to a low heat, spread the asparagus on the base and dry carefully for about 30 seconds. Arrange it on individual plates or in a serving dish and keep warm, or cool to room temperature.

3 To make the lemon-butter sauce, melt the butter in a small, heavy-based saucepan over a low heat. Whisk in the lemon juice and 2 tablespoons hot water. Season to taste.

4 Trickle a little sauce over the asparagus just before serving. Pour the rest into a warmed, small jug for people to help themselves.

VARIATIONS

● Halve the amount of lemon juice and use snipped fresh chervil or chives for a delicately-flavoured herb sauce.

● Add 1 tablespoon single cream or crème fraîche to the lemon butter sauce.

● Serve the sauce with steamed leeks, perhaps garnished with a finely chopped hard-boiled egg.

Mushroom Fricassée

THIS TRADITIONAL *French side dish can be served as a starter on a bed of salad leaves or to accompany an omelette.*

INGREDIENTS

1 tbsp olive oil

25g (1oz) butter

½ garlic clove

1 shallot, very finely chopped

400g (14oz) mixed mushrooms, sliced if large

salt and freshly ground black pepper

few sprigs of flat leaf parsley and chives

DICED BUTTER

VARIATION

To make a special brunch dish, add 1 tablespoon each of cream and port to the mushrooms towards the end of cooking. Serve on lightly toasted muffins.

1 Heat the oil with half the butter in a frying pan. Spear the garlic with a fork, rub around the hot pan, then discard or use in another dish. Add the shallot and cook, stirring, for 1 minute.

SHALLOTS

2 Spread the mushrooms in the pan. Season and cook over a medium heat, stirring frequently, for 5 minutes.

3 Stir the remaining butter into the mushrooms, then snip in a little parsley and some chives. Serve very hot on toasted muffins.

Potato Gratin

SLOW-COOKED POTATO DISHES *are typical of central and eastern France. This is a lighter version of creamy gratin dauphinois.*

INGREDIENTS

1 garlic clove, halved

50g (2oz) soft butter

900g (2lb) large, even-size waxy potatoes, thinly sliced

¼ tsp freshly grated nutmeg

cayenne pepper

salt and freshly ground black pepper

2 shallots, finely chopped

450ml (¾pint) hot vegetable stock

4½ tsp crème fraîche

serves 4 as a main course or 6–8 as side dish

POTATOES

1 Rub the cut sides of the garlic around a gratin dish that is large enough for four portions. Grease the dish well, using a third of the butter. Spread half the potatoes in the dish. Season with nutmeg, cayenne, salt and pepper.

2 Sprinkle over half the shallots, then dot with half the butter and pour over half the hot stock.

3 Repeat the layering, but omitting the butter. Pour over the remaining stock. Bake in a preheated oven at 180°C/350°F/gas 4 for 50 minutes, or until the potatoes are tender. Increase. the temperature to 200°C/400°F/gas 6.

4 Sprinkle the gratin with the crème fraîche, dot with the remaining butter and season with pepper. Bake for a further 10–15 minutes, or until bubbling and golden. Cool slightly before serving.

VARIATIONS

● Scatter a layer of sliced leeks and/or mushrooms between the potatoes.

● Replace the crème fraîche with 25g (1oz) crumbled blue cheese, grated Parmesan or Cheddar cheese.

Stuffed Tomatoes

AN OLD SUPPER FAVOURITE *in France, this satisfying dish takes a little time to prepare, but is worth the effort.*

INGREDIENTS

4 firm, ripe, large tomatoes

salt and freshly ground black pepper

2 garlic cloves, crushed

2 shallots, finely chopped

1 Spanish onion, finely chopped

2½ tbsp olive oil, plus extra for greasing

150g (5oz) button mushrooms, very thinly sliced

1 tsp dried thyme

½ tsp each dried oregano and savory or sage

5 tbsp breadcrumbs made from day-old wholemeal bread

2 tbsp pine nuts

1 large or 2 small eggs

l tsp sugar

a few drops of Tabasco sauce

50g (2oz) fresh goat's cheese

few sprigs of parsley, chives or basil, to garnish

1 Cut the tops off the tomatoes and reserve. Scoop out the seeds without breaking the skin; leave as much flesh as possible. Sprinkle salt in the cavities and invert on a plate lined with kitchen paper. Leave for 30 minutes.

PINE NUTS

2 Meanwhile, cook the garlic, shallots and onion in half the olive oil in a frying pan for 3 minutes. Add the mushrooms, thyme, oregano and savory and continue cooking for 3 minutes.

4 Squeeze the tomatoes very gently to drain, holding them upside down. Spoon in the filling without packing it too tightly. Top with the cheese and cover with the reserved tops. Put in a generously greased gratin dish and bake in a preheated oven at 190°C/375°F/gas 5 for 35–45 minutes, or until very tender. Leave to cool for at least 5 minutes before serving garnished with herbs on a bed of bulgar.

3 Stir in the breadcrumbs and pine nuts. Cook, stirring occasionally, for about 5 minutes. Season the mixture and tip into a bowl. Work in the egg, sugar and Tabasco.

Provençal Baked Vegetables

THIS FRAGRANT RECIPE *was traditionally cooked in an earthenware dish called a tian. It makes a good buffet party dish.*

INGREDIENTS

3–4 aubergines, thinly sliced

6 tbsp olive oil, plus extra for greasing

2 Spanish onions, chopped

2 garlic cloves, crushed

1 tsp each dried thyme, oregano and sage, mixed together

salt and freshly ground black pepper

6 tomatoes, sliced

2 courgettes, sliced

12 black olives, pitted and halved

1 orange or yellow pepper, charred (see page 14), sliced

3 tbsp grated Gruyère, Parmesan ewes' milk cheese, or crumbled goats' cheese

Serves 4 as a main course, 6 as a starter, or 8 as a side dish

1 Cook the aubergine slices in batches in 2 tablespoons of the olive oil in a large frying pan until browned; add more oil as necessary. Remove the slices to a double layer of kitchen paper and drain well.

2 Fry the onion, garlic and some of the herbs for a few minutes, until softened. Season.

3 Spread a layer of aubergine in a lightly oiled gratin dish. Season lightly and sprinkle with a few dried herbs. Add the tomatoes, then the courgettes and the onion mixture.

4 Scatter over the black olives. Season, sprinkle with herbs. Cover with the pepper strips. Add more herbs. Finish with aubergines, a sprinkling of herbs and a little more olive oil.

5 Bake in a preheated oven at 180°C/350°F/gas 4 for 30 minutes. Press lightly with a slotted spoon and scoop off the moisture. Sprinkle over the cheese. Increase the heat to 200°C/400°F/gas 6 and bake for a further 15 minutes. Serve warm or at room temperature.

SLICED
COURGETTES

Green Beans with Parsley and Almonds

GREEN BEANS *are a favourite vegetable in France. Here they are enhanced with almonds, parsley and a little garlic.*

INGREDIENTS

450g (1lb) green beans, topped and tailed

salt and freshly ground black pepper

1 garlic clove, crushed

1 tbsp olive oil

20g (¾oz) butter

3 tbsp flaked almonds

3 tbsp finely snipped parsley

COOK'S TIP

This recipe makes a good accompaniment to Stuffed Tomatoes (see page 40) or Tomato Tart (see page 32).

GREEN BEANS WITH PARSLEY AND ALMONDS

1 Cook the beans in a large saucepan of boiling, salted water until just tender; small beans will take 5–6 minutes, larger ones will take about 8–9 minutes. Drain in a colander and refresh under cold water. Drain again.

3 Scatter the almonds into the pan and cook, stirring constantly, for 1 minute.

2 Cook the garlic in the oil and half the butter in a frying pan over a medium heat for a few seconds.

4 Spread in the beans. Turn up the heat a little and cook for 2 minutes. Sprinkle over the parsley. Stir in the remaining butter, taste and adjust the seasoning, if necessary. Serve hot.

Stuffed Cabbage with Red Pepper Sauce

THESE TASTY PARCELS, *or* paupiettes, *are filled with a well-seasoned stuffing and steamed to make a healthy main course.*

INGREDIENTS

12 outer leaves from a large
Savoy cabbage

5 tbsp olive oil

40 g (1½oz) butter

2 each spring onions and shallots,
finely chopped

1 red pepper, finely chopped

150g (5oz) button mushrooms,
finely sliced

1½ garlic cloves, crushed

½ tsp each ground cumin, ground
coriander and grated lemon rind

¼ tsp harissa or chilli paste

4½ tsp plump raisins

2 tbsp chopped shelled pistachio nuts

115g/7oz prepared couscous

1 large egg

bouquet garni

FOR THE SAUCE

2 large red peppers, charred and peeled
(see page 14)

½ tsp dried oregano

a few basil leaves

salt and freshly ground black pepper

1 tbsp each cream and yogurt

1 Cook the cabbage for 2 minutes in salted boiling water. Plunge into cold water, drain and dry on kitchen paper. Cut out the tough stalks.

46

STUFFED CABBAGE WITH RED PEPPER SAUCE

2 Cook the spring onions, shallots, red pepper, mushrooms, 1 garlic clove, the cumin, coriander, harissa or chilli paste, lemon rind, raisins and pistachio nuts in 1 tablespoon oil and half the butter for 5 minutes, stirring frequently. Tip into a bowl. Stir in the couscous, egg and seasoning, mixing well.

3 Spoon some stuffing on to the centre of each cabbage leaf. Roll the leaves into neat parcels and secure with string.

4 Boil 600ml (1 pint) water with the bouquet garni. Place the parcels in a steamer on top; dot with the remaining butter. Cover and steam for 30 minutes. Discard the strings.

5 Meanwhile, purée the peeled peppers, remaining oil and garlic, oregano, basil leaves and seasoning. Stir in the cream and yogurt. Tip into a sauceboat. Rinse the processor with 6 tablespoons water, then stir into the sauceboat. Serve with the cabbage parcels.

Warm Green Lentil Salad

THE SMALL GREEN LENTILS *grown around the town of Le Puy in central France have a subtle nutty flavour and are highly nutritious.*

INGREDIENTS

350g (12oz) Le Puy lentils or other green or brown lentils

1 bouquet garni

several sprigs of flat leaf parsley

3 tbsp olive oil

½ tsp dried sage

1 large spring onion, finely chopped

1 tbsp sherry vinegar

salt and freshly ground black pepper

2 Drain off excess liquid (use for a soup or stock) and discard the bouquet garni.

1 Simmer the lentils and bouquet garni in a large, uncovered saucepan of water for 25–35 minutes, or until the lentils are just tender.

SPRING ONIONS

3 Meanwhile, snip the parsley into a small bowl. Add the oil, sage, spring onion and sherry vinegar. Stir well to mix and season to taste.

4 Tip the cooked lentils into a bowl, spoon over the dressing and toss lightly to coat. Serve the salad warm or at room temperature.

Peas Braised with Lettuce

THIS LOVELY RECIPE *is an excellent unfussy way to cook fresh, tender young peas. Use chervil instead of parsley if you can get it.*

INGREDIENTS

4 leaves from a soft lettuce, shredded

1 spring onion, white part only, finely chopped

450g (1lb) shelled small garden peas, about 1.75 kg (4lb) unshelled weight

40g (1½oz) butter

pinch of sugar

2 sprigs of flat leaf parsley, plus extra to garnish

salt and freshly ground black pepper

1 Stir the lettuce and spring onion into half the butter in a sauté pan over a medium heat.

2 Add the peas, sugar and parsley to the pan.

3 Season lightly and pour in enough water to cover. Bring to a simmer, reduce the heat a little, cover and cook until the peas are just tender; depending on the peas, this will take 10–15 minutes.

4 Drain the vegetables, then transfer to a warmed serving dish. Stir in the remaining butter and sprinkle over the extra parsley to garnish. Serve immediately.

GARDEN
PEAS

COOK'S TIP

Use frozen peas, but replace the water with a light stock and stir in a tablespoon of cream at the end to enhance them.

Parsleyed Broccoli and Cauliflower

THE BREADCRUMB AND PARSLEY *mixture used here, known as* persillade, *can be used to finish any plain vegetable dish.*

INGREDIENTS

1 cauliflower, cut in small florets

salt and freshly ground black pepper

2 broccoli heads, cut in small florets

1 garlic clove, crushed

25g (1oz) breadcrumbs made from day-old bread

25g (1oz) butter

3 tbsp finely chopped parsley

CAULIFLOWER

PARSLEY

1 Cook the cauliflower in boiling, salted water for 5 minutes. Add the broccoli and cook for 5 minutes more, or until almost tender.

2 Drain the vegetables. Arrange attractively on a heatproof plate, alternating broccoli and cauliflower. Season lightly and keep warm.

3 Cook the garlic and crumbs in the butter in a small frying pan over a medium heat for 1–2 minutes, or until golden. Add the parsley and stir for another minute. Spoon over the florets. Serve hot. ′

Caramelized Upside Down Apple Tart

THIS GOLDEN TART, *known as* tarte tatin, *is a classic from the Sologne area near Orleans. It should have a slightly burnt finish.*

INGREDIENTS

800g (1¾lb) crisp eating apples, peeled, cored and quartered

130g (4½oz) unsalted butter

150g (5oz) caster sugar, plus 1 tbsp for sprinkling

FOR THE PASTRY

225g (8oz) plain flour

1 tbsp caster sugar

salt

130g (4½oz) chilled unsalted butter, cut into slivers

1 tbsp chilled single cream

Serves 6–8

1 To make the pastry, stir the flour, sugar and salt together. Rub in the butter, then mix in the cream. Form into a ball. Chill for 20 minutes.

APPLE SLICES

2 Melt half the butter in a flameproof 20cm (8in) cake tin over a medium heat. Stir in half the sugar. Cook for 5 minutes, or until just golden.

3 Off the heat, arrange the apples in tight circles in the tin, starting from the outside. Add the remaining sugar and butter.

4 Return to a medium heat for 15–20 minutes, or until the apples are tender and the butter and sugar have caramelized. If they brown too quickly, reduce the heat. Shake the tin occasionally. Leave the tin until cool enough to handle.

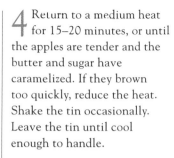

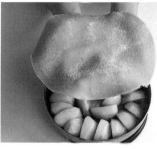

5 Roll out the pastry to a thin 24cm (9½in) circle. Sprinkle with the extra sugar, pressing it in gently. Place the pastry, sugar side down, over the apples. Tuck the overhang between the apples and tin. Bake in a preheated oven at 200°C/400°F/gas 6 for about 25–30 minutes, or until golden. Cool for 10 minutes. Cover with a serving plate and invert the tart on to the plate, so that the apples are on top. Tap the tin a few times and lift it off.

Poached Cherries

SERVED WITH FROMAGE FRAIS *or ricotta cheese, this colourful combination is popular in the Basque region, as well as south and west of the Pyrenees.*

INGREDIENTS

450g (1lb) cherries, pitted
60g/2½oz unsalted butter
4 tbsp caster sugar
6 tbsp orange juice
3 tbsp lemon juice
3 tbsp crème de cassis
fromage frais or ricotta cheese, to serve
12 whole cherries, to decorate

1 Gently cook the cherries in the butter, sugar, orange juice, lemon juice and 6–7 tablespoons water in a heavy-based saucepan, stirring gently several times, for about 7–10 minutes.

VARIATION

Replace the scoops of fromage frais with the whole cherries coated in fromage frais or ricotta cheese. Serve with the poached cherries.

ORANGE JUICE

2 Drain the cherries over a bowl. Reserve the cherries and return the liquid to the pan. Boil until reduced by about one-third.

3 Stir in the crème de cassis, then bubble for 1 minute. Serve the cherries with scoops of fromage frais. Spoon over the sauce just before serving.

Regional variations

FRANCE STRETCHES *from the temperate lands of north-west Europe to the sunny olive-producing shores of the Mediterranean. The produce and cooking reflect these very different climates.*

In the fertile dairy regions of western France, the local cheeses are rich and made from cows' milk, and the preferred cooking fats are cream and unsalted butter; the exception is Brittany, where salted butter is used.

South of Brittany and Normandy the western Loire is rich in market gardens and many different goats'

GOATS' CHEESE cheeses. Further south, with the warmer climate, there are plenty of early season fruit producers, and fragrant herbs grow plentifully on the hillsides. Local cheeses are made from goats' milk or ewes' milk and tend to be drier than those of the north-west.

Olive oil is used as the main cooking fat, and a great variety of olives are eaten. The principal vegetables are those of the rest of southern Europe: aubergines, tomatoes, peppers and courgettes.

SLICED COURGETTES

Further north along the eastern side of France, past the windy, warm orchards and market gardens of the Rhône, the climate becomes more harsh. In this area lentils, root vegetables, herbs and hard cheeses are used to prepare hearty, dishes.

TARRAGON

BLACK OLIVES

Further reading

EDIBLE FRANCE, *Glyn Christian*
(Grub Street, 1996)

COOKING OF SOUTHWEST FRANCE,
Paula Wolfert (Grub Street, 1999)

FRENCH VEGETARIAN COOKBOOK,
Paola Gavin (Optima, 1994)

VEGETARIAN BISTRO, *Marlene Spieler*
(Chronicle, 1997)

FRANCE: THE VEGETARIAN TABLE,
Georgeann Brennan (Chronicle, 1995)

FRENCH COUNTRY COOKING,
Elizabeth David (Penguin, 1959)

FRENCH PROVINCIAL COOKING,
Elizabeth David (Penguin, 1986)

BISTRO COOKING, *Patricia Wells*
(Kyle Cathie, 1999)

THE ESSENTIAL PROVENCE COOKBOOK
(Hamlyn, 1999)

THE FLAVOURS OF FRANCE, *Jean Conil*
(Angus & Robertson, 1995)

Useful addresses

The Vegetarian Society
Parkdale
Durham Road
Altrincham
Cheshire WA14 4QG
UK

**The Vegetarian Union
of North America**
PO Box 9710
Washington DC 20016
USA

**The Australian
Vegetarian Society**
PO Box 65
2021 Paddington
Australia

The Soil Association
86 Colston Street
Bristol BS1 5BB
UK

Farm Verified Organic
RR 1
Box 40A USA
Medina
ND 58467
USA

**National Association for
Sustainable Agriculture**
PO Box 768
AUS-Sterling
SA 5152
Australia